WhAT'S THE BiG IDEA?

Activities and Adventures in ABSTRACT ART

by Ryan, 8

JOYCE RAIMONDO

Watson-Guptill Publications/New York

For my loving friends: Lenore Bingham, Michele Cavalier, Hope Finkelstein, Pearl Golden, Brenda Kelly, Robin Laban, Rosemary Markowsky, and my sister, Mary Berry, with gratitude

by Lucas, 8

Copyright © 2008 by Joyce Raimondo
First published in 2008 by Watson-Guptill Publications
Nielsen Business Media, a division of The Nielsen Company
770 Broadway, New York, NY 10003
www.watsonguptill.com

Step-by-step artwork by Joyce Raimondo. Photographs of three-dimensional art by Frank Roccanova. Author photo on page 48 by Kathleen Bifulco.

Picture credits: **Page 8**: *Weeping Woman,* 1937, by Pablo Picasso (1881–1973). Oil on canvas, size 19.7 x 23.9 inches (500 x 608 mm). Copyright © Tate, London 2007. © 2007 Estate of Pablo Picasso / Artists Rights Society (ARS), New York. **Page 14**: *The City,* 1919, by Fernand Léger. Philadelphia Museum of Art; A.E. Gallatin Collection, 1952, 1952-61-58. © 2007 Artists Rights Society (ARS), New York / ADAGP, Paris. **Page 20 and cover**: *Jazz,* 1947, by Henri Matisse (1869–1954). Color pochoir; lithographed text; artist's book. 16 ½ x 12 ¾ inches (41.91 x 32.39 cm). Minneapolis Institute of Arts, Gift of Bruce B. Dayton, B.82.1. © 2007 Succession H. Matisse, Paris / Artists Rights Society (ARS), New York. **Page 26**: *Myxomatose,* 1953, by Alexander Calder (1898–1976). Sheet metal, rod, wire, and paint, 256.5 x 408.9 cm (101 x 161 inches). Private collection. Art Resource, New York. Copyright © ARS, NY. © 2007 Calder Foundation, New York / Artists Rights Society (ARS), New York. **Page 32**: *Red Canna,* c. 1923, by Georgia O'Keeffe (American, 1887–1986). Oil on canvas mounted on masonite. 36 x 29 ⅞ inches (91.4 x 76.0 cm). Collection of The University of Arizona Museum of Art, Tucson, Gift of Oliver James. Acc. No. 50.1.4. © 2007 Georgia O'Keeffe Museum / Artists Rights Society (ARS), New York. **Page 38**: *Water of the Flowery Mill,*1944, by Arshile Gorky (1904–1948). Oil on canvas, H. 42-¼, W. 48-¾ inches (107.3 x 123.8 cm)/The Metropolitan Museum of Art, George A. Hearn Fund, 1956 (56.205.1). Image copyright © The Metropolitan Museum of Art. © 2007 Artists Rights Society (ARS), New York

Every effort has been made to ensure accuracy in this book and to acknowledge all copyright holders. We will be pleased to correct any inadvertent errors or omissions in future editions.

ISBN-13: 978-1-8230-9998-6
ISBN-10: 1-8230-9998-9
Library of Congress Control Number: 2007935507

Senior Acquisitions Editor: Julie Mazur
Project Editor: Laaren Brown
Designer: Edward Miller
Production Manager: Salvatore Destro
The typefaces in this book include Futura, Typography of Coop, and Ad Lib.

Manufactured in Malaysia
First printing, 2008
1 2 3 4 5 6 7 / 14 13 12 11 10 09 08

Contents

by Hannah, 9

Help Your Child Explore Abstract Art

What's the Big Idea? invites children to **explore abstract art** and use it as a springboard for their own creativity. The discussions in this book encourage children to **examine works of art** and **develop their own personal interpretations**. Related projects encourage children to create their own art inspired by the famous artists' ideas and techniques.

What do you see in this picture?

Bright exploding **colors**! Wild **lines**! Playful **shapes** that flow across the painting! What do you **see**? What do you **imagine**? The questions in this book **motivate creative thinking** by asking children to describe and interpret what they see. Let go of your own ideas and **affirm the children's insights**. In a group, **encourage different opinions**. Older children may want to research the artists' lives, and they can start with the biographies in this book.

Create your own abstract art

Some abstract artists paint the world they **observe** around them—people, places, and things—using simplified or exaggerated forms. Others delve inside their **imagination** and release their inner **feelings** in abstract paintings and sculptures. *What's the Big Idea?* invites children to do the same: to **express themselves freely** by playing with shapes, lines, and colors. Some of the projects ask children to try actual working methods of artists, such as Matisse-inspired cutouts. Other projects, such as printing geometric patterns, explore abstract art concepts with materials adapted for children.

Spark your imagination

Begin your exploration of abstract art with a **lively conversation**. Discuss the famous pictures in this book. Visit a local museum, too. You can also **spark ideas** by relating the art projects to your **child's experience**. For example, to explore shapes, ask your child to find geometric shapes in the room or patterns on clothing.

Everyone is creative

The art instructions guide young artists on **a journey of discovery**. Do not expect children to follow them exactly. Demonstrate techniques, such as how to make a print or construct a mobile. Then let kids work with a spirit of experimentation. **Everyone has his or her own way of making art**, and creativity is a gift to be nurtured in everyone.

by Nicole, 10

An Adventure in Abstract Art

Bold, beautiful, baffling! This book highlights six abstract artists whose groundbreaking work revolutionized art. Instead of telling stories in painting, abstract artists explore the elements of art—line, shape, color, pattern, texture, and form—as subjects in their own right. In some of their artworks, you might recognize a figure, a place, or an object that has been abstracted by simplifying or exaggerating its form. In pure abstraction, or non-objective art, the work does not make reference to anything outside itself.

As a museum educator, I have observed that while adults are often mystified by abstract art, children are open to all different kinds of art and are eager to discuss abstract pictures. For this book, I have chosen popular abstract artworks that suggest representational subjects through a variety of styles. Their dramatic imagery and playful techniques pique a child's curiosity.

In Pablo Picasso's *Weeping Woman*, the artist projected his own strong feelings in an Expressionist portrait. A Cubist painter, Picasso shows multiple views in one picture. It is as if you are seeing a face in motion, or moving through and around it. Influenced by Picasso, Fernand Léger captured the energy of modern life in his Cubist city painting.

Henri Matisse created joyful shapes and patterns in his colorful cutouts. He eliminated nonessential details to capture the essence of his subjects. In response to his bold colors, Matisse became known as a Fauve painter, from the French word for "wild beasts."

For Alexander Calder, lines and shapes took three-dimensional form. The inventor of the mobile, Calder chose movement itself as the subject of his dynamic sculptures.

Georgia O'Keeffe drew upon her keen observations of nature as a springboard for intuitive abstract images. In her popular flower paintings, she paints larger-than-life blossoms filled with sensual lines and colors.

Also inspired by nature, Arshile Gorky expressed his emotions by letting paint drip and colors explode onto his canvases. In contrast to the hard-edged paintings of Picasso and Leger, Gorky and the Abstract Expressionists released their energy with painterly brushstrokes and fluid paint.

Additional activities in Abstract Expressionism are presented in my book *Express Yourself*; Surrealist approaches are included in *Imagine That*. Playful, imaginative, and expressive, abstract artists courageously show us what creativity is all about!

Be an Abstract Artist!

Welcome to the amazing world of **abstract art**! Instead of making everything look real, abstract artists use **bold colors, shapes, and lines** to make exciting art. In some abstract pictures, you might see funny faces or mixed-up places. In other abstract art, you might not recognize anything at all. **Look** at the art in this book. Talk about what you **see** and **imagine**. Then create your own **abstract art**.

In this book, you will see how abstract artists show their **feelings**. Meet a sad, crying woman with a green face filled with **sharp, pointy shapes**. Go to a circus where **happy cutout shapes** fly across the picture. Then create your own **colorful cutouts** to tell how *you* feel!

Visit an **abstract city** made of **geometric shapes**. A rectangle might be a tall building. A circle might be a sun. You will see playful **patterns**, too. Look around! Mix up the shapes in your world and turn them into art. Why not put a pink building and green stripes in the air?

Learn how artists get ideas from looking at **nature**. See a gigantic flower filled with **beautiful designs**. Travel

by Alexandra, 12

by Jake, 11

on a river that overflows into a garden of exploding colors. Try it yourself! Change your favorite flowers, seashells, or anything else into gorgeous designs.

Discover what modern **sculpture** is all about. Build with wire, straws, sticks, beads, and more to create an abstract animal or fun-filled form. Add stuff you find around your home. Make a **mobile**, and watch it move!

Dive into your **imagination**. Let lines and colors **flow freely** from your hand. Make a **messy** painting—splash, spill, and scrape into paint. **Surprise yourself!**

Explore your **creativity**. There is no such thing as a mistake in art. **Play** with shapes, colors, lines, patterns, and forms! Discover all the **exciting** ways you can make **abstract art**!

7

by Caitlin, 12

WEIRD, WILD FACES

PABLO PICASSO

Picture a woman with a green face! That's what the artist Pablo Picasso did when he painted this picture of his girlfriend, Dora Maar. As you can see, Picasso did not paint his girlfriend the way she really looked. In real life, Dora was beautiful. Instead of painting her features, Picasso painted this portrait to show how the woman felt on the inside. Tears flow from her shattered eyes. The jagged shapes all over her face look sharp, like broken glass.

This unusual face seems all mixed up. Is her nose on the side of her head or in the middle of her face? Her eyes seem to be in the wrong places. Fingers are everywhere. Picasso captured the woman's head and hands moving all around as she sobs. Picasso created this style of abstract art that shows more than one viewpoint, called Cubism.

When Picasso painted this picture, his country, Spain, was at war. People were hurting one another. Picasso was enraged. He made many imaginative pictures of weeping women to express his strong emotions.

How do you think this **woman feels**? How can you tell?

- What is **unusual** about the weeping woman's **eyes**? How would you describe them? Look closely at the shapes of her eyes. What else could they be?
- Look at her **mouth**. What do you notice? What might those lines next to her mouth be?
- Notice her **ear**. What seems **odd** about it? Why do you think it looks that way?
- Find her **fingers**. What do you think she is doing with her **hands**?

- Notice the **large white shapes** in the center of her face. What might they be?
- The name of this picture is *Weeping Woman*. How many **tears** can you find? Take a **second look**. What else might the **tears** be?
- The face seems **mixed up**. Where is the woman's **nose**? Can you find it in more than one place? What else seems **strange** about this face?
- What **shapes** do you see in this face ? Can you find a **triangle**? An **oval**? A **diamond**? Why would Picasso make the shapes of the face so **sharp**?

Weeping Woman, 1937
oil on canvas, 19.7 x 23.9 inches
Tate Gallery, London, England

Imagine. Why is the woman crying? Make up a story about the *Weeping Woman*.

Express your feelings!
Discover creative ways to make abstract faces inspired by Picasso.

Feeling Faces

Make art inspired by Picasso

Make an abstract mask that shows a feeling using cut-paper shapes and paint. Like Picasso, instead of making a person who looks real, use abstract shapes to show an emotion. An angry person might be filled with sharp, jagged shapes. A silly face can be made of curly shapes. Be creative. Mix it all up. You can put the eyes and nose in the wrong place!

1. What feeling will you show? Make a face that's silly, angry, happy, sad, scared, confused, or one that shows any other emotion.

2. Make the face with large colored shapes. Use colors to show a feeling. Red and black might look mad. My yellow-and-orange face looks cheerful to me.

3. Cut out shapes for the eyes, nose, and mouth. Instead of making the features look real, cut shapes to show a feeling. A zigzag mouth might show anger. I cut curvy shapes and spirals for a silly, happy face.

4. Add designs. Cut out wrapping paper. Move your shapes around. When you are ready, glue your papers.

5. Add finishing touches. Paint designs and patterns.

6. Make the mask. Glue your picture to a sheet of cardboard. Tape a cardboard strip to the back for a handle. Hold your mask in front of your face. See if people can guess the feeling you created.

Supplies

Construction paper
Decorative paper
Scissors
Glue
Paint supplies
Cardboard

Crazy colorful face.—Rachel, 10

Face of fear.—Priyanka, 10

So silly!—Josephine, 10

Try this, too!

Recycled Masks

Picasso loved to find old junk and use it to make art. Once he found an old toy car and made it into the face of a baboon! Collect old toys, bottle caps, buttons, ribbons, wrapping paper, or anything else. Glue colorful papers to a sheet of cardboard to make a face. Then glue on stuff for the eyes, nose, mouth, ears, and hair. (Ask an adult to use a hot-glue gun for plastic pieces.) Recycle for art!

Silly pink ice-cream nose. —Sarah, 8

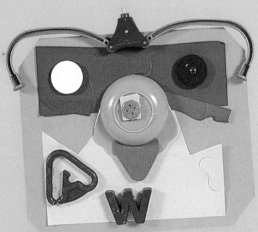

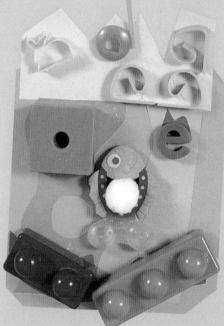

Mixed-up emotions!—Lucas, 8

Mix It Up!

Another Picasso idea

Paint a Cubist face using oil pastels and tempera. Look at the *Weeping Woman* on page 9. Her eyes are facing forward, yet her nose is seen in profile on the side of her head. Look again. You might also see her nose in the middle of her face. Picasso showed many viewpoints in this Cubist picture. It is as if the woman's head is moving all around. Try it yourself. Draw different viewpoints in one crazy face!

1. Look at a person's face from different viewpoints.
What does a person look like from the side? From the front?

2. Draw a face in profile. I drew the nose the way it looks when a person is seen from the side. I added lips and an eye.

3. Add other features facing forward. Draw a nose seen from the front. Add an eye and another mouth.

4. Mix it up. You can draw funny eyes and lips in the wrong places. I drew one circle eye and two lips.

5. Add fun designs. Draw colorful crazy hair. Add shapes on the face. (Tip: As you draw, press hard with your oil pastels so the lines show up.)

6. Paint a colorful face. Thin your paint by adding water. Paint lightly at first, so your lines will show up. After your painting dries, draw back over your lines if needed. Do not forget to paint the background, too.

Supplies

White paper
Oil pastels
Tempera or watercolor
paint supplies

Every child is an artist. The problem is how to remain an artist once he grows up. —Pablo Picasso

Crying girl.—Amy, 10

Cute and colorful.—Kerri, 10

Funny lady!—Erica, 10

Looking at you?—Jake, 11

Fierce face.—Allie, 10

Try this, too!

It's All in Your Head!

What would it be like if you had eyes in the back of your head or a nose on the side of your face? Would you like to have purple eyes and orange skin? Picasso painted and sculpted hundreds of creative heads. With self-hardening clay, mold a ball for a head. Then add unusual eyes, a nose, lips, and ears anyplace you want. Squeeze clay through a garlic press for hair. When your creation is dry, paint it fun colors. Anything goes!

Funny face.—Emma, 8

WORLD OF SHAPES

FERNAND LÉGER

Welcome to a wonderful world of city shapes, created by the artist Fernand Léger. When Léger painted this picture, he lived in the big city of Paris, France. Instead of making everything look real, with buildings on the ground and the sun in the sky, Léger captured the exciting energy of the modern city in this abstract picture. Geometric shapes, bold colors, and patterns flash across the painting in a lively, fun-filled design.

Look closely. You will see so many things in this city: posters, signs, bridges, buildings, streets, and more. Two people who look like robots walk up the stairs. Follow them into the picture. Imagine what it would be like in this place. Bright contrasting colors show us this is an active, noisy city. As in Picasso's painting on page 9, everything in this Cubist city picture seems to be moving and shifting all around. After Léger made this painting in 1919, his masterpiece traveled from city to city, and he became famous for it.

What **place** might this be? How can you tell?

- **Imagine** being in this picture. What would it be like? How would you **describe** this place? Is it quiet or noisy, lively or still, fun or scary?
- Look closely. Can you find **a street, a building, a bridge**, or **a sign**? What other things do you see?
- How many **people** can you find? How would you describe them? **Who** might they be? What might they be **doing**?
- Play a **looking game**. What **shapes** do you see? What **circles, rectangles**, and **squares** can you find? Can you find a **semi-circle**, a **triangle**, a **diamond**? What other shapes can you find?
- How many **patterns** can you find? A pattern is made when a

The City, 1919
oil on canvas, 91 x 117 inches
Philadelphia Museum of Art

shape is repeated over and over. Can you find
stripes, dashes, a crisscross?

- Can you find **letters of the alphabet**? Why do you think they
are in the picture?
- Look at the **entire picture**. Make up a **title** for it. Why would
you call it that?

The artist called his picture *The City*. How is this **different**
from a real city? What about it is **similar**?

What shapes are in your world? Make
abstract pictures filled with geometric shapes and patterns.

City Shapes

Make art inspired by Léger

Make an abstract collage of a city filled with geometric shapes and patterns. Léger loved the lively shapes and patterns he saw around him in the city of Paris. He painted them in his abstract pictures. Look around. Notice all the rectangles, squares, and circles you see around you every day! Then cut and paste shapes and patterns to create your own abstract place.

1. Play a looking game. What geometric shapes do you see? What things are rectangles or circles? Can you find triangles, diamonds, or ovals? What patterns do you see?

2. Paint patterned paper. I painted stripes, polka dots, and checkers. Let the paint dry. Cut out these shapes to use in your project later. You can also collect papers that have patterns on them.

3. First, paste large colored shapes on your picture.

4. Cut out shapes of buildings, roads, and other things you find in a city. I made a rectangle building with a triangle roof. I cut out a semicircle for a tunnel.

5. Mix it up! Do not put everything on the ground. Instead, make a lively abstract picture. I pasted a checkered pattern and wavy lines in the background.

6. Create patterns. Repeat the same shape over and over. I added colorful squares for a fun pattern. Cut up your patterned papers, too.

7. Add details. Circles make the wheels of a car. A square makes a door. You can also add letters of the alphabet with stickers. As you work, move your shapes around. At the end, glue them down.

Supplies

Colored paper
Patterned papers
Paint supplies
Glue
Scissors

In *The City,...*color had become free. It was a reality in its own right. It had a new activity independent of the objects which had contained it.—Fernand Léger

Stop and go.—Zachary, 9

Funky town.—Alexandra, 12

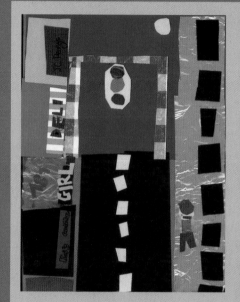

Shop in the city.—Katie, 9

Driving through town.—Alyssa, 11

Try this, too!

Tape it! Shape It!

Léger's painting is filled with shapes that are carefully painted in. This kind of painting is called hard-edge painting. The famous artist Piet Mondrian also made hard-edge shape paintings. Mondrian made neat lines and shapes by using tape. Make your own tape painting. You will need glossy poster board and painter's tape. Tape lines across your board to create shapes. Then paint colors right over your tape. When the paint is dry, carefully peel off the tape. Surprise!

Confusing colors.—Emma, 8

Shape Prints

Make patterns inspired by Léger

Print out geometric shapes and patterns using collograph printmaking. Stripes, zigzags, and dashes! Circles, diamonds, and squares! Can you find these in Léger's painting on page 15? Now create designs of your own. For this project, instead of painting your shapes and patterns, print them out. This kind of print—when you roll ink onto materials and use them to make a new image—is called a collograph.

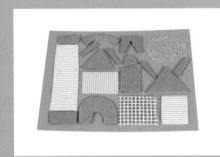

1. Cut out geometric shapes from cardboard. (You can ask an adult to help.) I cut out circles, squares, rectangles, and ovals.

2. Gather textured materials that have patterns on them. Bubble wrap has a dot design. A screen has a grid. Corrugated paper is striped. Run your fingers along the material to feel the designs. Cut out shapes from these materials.

3. Glue your shapes on a board. You can make a busy city picture or an abstract design. Wait for the glue to dry. (Tip: Place shapes next to one another; *do not overlap*.)

4. Carefully roll ink onto the shapes with a brayer (roller). Try not to get the ink onto the empty spaces of your board.

5. Place a sheet of paper over the shapes. Gently press with your hand or a brayer.

6. Surprise! Lift up the paper to see your print.

7. Copy it! Repeat the process to print more pictures. Experiment with different kinds of papers. You can also roll out different colors of ink to get different effects.

Supplies

Water-based printing ink
Brayer (roller)
Textured materials, like
    bubble wrap,
    corrugated paper,
    screen

Cardboard shapes
Cardboard for base
Scissors
Glue
Paper

Shapes in town.—Courtney, 8

Colorful buildings.—Alex, 8

Sun and moon over the city.—Fred, 8

Try this, too!

Stamp It Out

Léger became famous for his colorful paintings that were filled with patterns. Look for patterns in your home or on the street. Are you wearing any patterns? Use sponge painting to make an abstract city or design that is filled with patterns. First, cut sponges into shapes or buy precut shapes. Pour paint on a paper plate, then dip your sponge into it. Stamp, stamp, stamp! What patterns will you create?

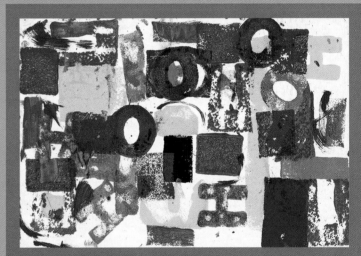

What shapes do you see?—Kevin, 10

Windy city.—Chris, 11

COLORFUL CUTOUTS

HENRI MATISSE

Wiggly shapes that dance and float! Bright bursts of color! When the artist Henri Matisse made this bold abstract picture, he was remembering the circus and his travels. The colorful shapes that fly across the picture might be trapeze performers or circus animals. Look at all the black squares. Are those the audience or a net below the flying acrobats?

Matisse made this picture by cutting out stencils and printing through them with paint. Then he assembled different printed cutouts in a beautiful handmade book called *Jazz*. Matisse first began making colorful cutouts when he grew old. Bedridden, he could no longer paint. Matisse did not give up. Working from bed, he cut painted papers into shapes. His assistant pinned the papers loosely on the walls all around him. Then Matisse arranged the shapes in colorful collages and glued them down. Matisse called this way of making art "drawing with scissors." His paper cutouts and stenciled prints, made in his eighties, are some of his greatest masterpieces.

Look at these **colorful cutouts**. What do you **see**?

- What do all the **shapes and colors** remind you of? What makes you say that?
- **Imagine.** Notice all the red and blue **wobbly shapes**. What might those be?
- Find a blue **rectangular** shape and a white one. What could these be?
- What might all those **black squares** be?
- When Matisse made this **colorful** picture, he was inspired by his memories of the **circus**. What in the picture might show a circus?
- Can you find a shape that that looks like an **acrobat**? A

The Codomas (Les Codomas),
Plate XI from *Jazz*, 1947. Color pochoir, lithographed text.
Artist's book, 16 x 12 inches. Minneapolis Institute of Arts

trapeze? Do you see circus **animals** or **performers**?
What else do you see in this picture?

- What, if anything, seems to be **moving** in this picture?
- What is the **feeling** or **mood** in this picture? What makes you say that?
- How would you describe the shapes in this picture? Which shapes are **geometric**? Can you find the same shape repeated over and over to form a **pattern**?

Compare this picture to Picasso's *Weeping Woman*. How are the two pictures **different**? What is **similar** about them?

Have fun with cutouts!
Like Matisse, make happy art filled
with bold shapes and bright colors.

21

Draw with Scissors

Create cutouts like Matisse

Make a joyful collage using colorful cutout shapes. Matisse wanted his art to be happy. In his cutouts, he pictured a fun-filled circus, dancers, swimmers, animals, music, and more. Instead of making everything look real, Matisse made abstract collages by gluing flowing shapes, patterns, and bold colors. Like Matisse, get out your scissors and create a joyful cutout.

1. Choose a subject. What makes you happy? You can make a circus, a dance, the seaside, a sport, a colorful garden, or a joyful abstract design. I made a silly circus.

2. Create a background. Like Matisse, first cut and paste large colorful shapes.

3. Think about what you might find in your place. For my circus, I imagined jugglers and dancing clowns. What will you put in your picture?

4. Make it abstract. Cut out flowing shapes for your scene. (Flowing shapes like these, which look as if they come from nature, are called organic shapes.) Do not draw first—cut right into the paper with scissors.

5. Use the leftover papers. When I cut out my clown, the hole in the paper also made a shape. I put that in my scene, too. Can you find it?

6. Make patterns and designs. Cut out the same shape more than once to create patterns. I made colorful circles that fly around.

7. Make it colorful. Like Matisse, change the colors of everything. I made a green-and-yellow clown floating in pink air.

8. Glue down your shapes at the end.

Supplies

Colored paper
Scissors
Glue

Amazing ocean.—Brianna, 8

Try this, too!

Puzzle Pictures

When Matisse cut out paper shapes, he noticed that the leftover scraps made beautiful shapes, too. Discover all the amazing shapes you can make using only two colors of paper. Here are some ideas: Fold a sheet of paper in half. Cut a shape around the fold. Open it. The shape of the "hole" is called a negative shape. Paste it down. Glue the leftover scrap papers, too. Overlap your shapes. Make patterns. What kinds of shapes will you create?

I love soccer!—Emily, 10

Why listen to the radio when you can make one?—Sierra, 8

Fun-filled circus.—Ryan, 8

What I dream of is an art of balance of purity and serenity...a soothing, calming influence on the mind, something like a good armchair which provides relaxation from physical fatigue.—Henri Matisse

Playful Prints

More art inspired by Matisse

Using foam printing, make a picture filled with lively patterns.

Matisse made copies of his colorful picture on page 21 by printing it out with stencils. Then he assembled his prints in his own handmade book. It is fun to make copies of your pictures. This project shows you an easy way to print out bold shapes. Fill your picture with playful patterns and fun designs.

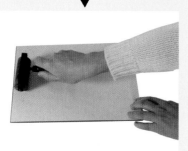

1. First, make a simple collage. Glue a few large colored-paper shapes to your paper. Put the paper aside to dry. (You will print over this later.)

2. Make your printing plate. Cut foam into shapes. I made wobbly shapes and circles. Glue them to a sheet of cardboard. (Tip: Do not overlap shapes. Glue shapes next to one another.)

3. Cut out foam patterns. Cut the same shape several times. Glue down the foam shapes.

4. Carefully roll ink onto the foam shapes with a brayer (roller). Try not to get the ink onto the empty spaces of your board. (Tip: Cover up any wet ink that got on the cardboard with small newspaper scraps.)

5. Place your collage over your printing plate face down. Keeping it in place, gently rub the entire paper with your hand or a brayer.

6. Lift up the paper to see your print. (Tip: You can touch up your shapes using a paintbrush and ink if you want.)

7. Copy it! Repeat the process to print more pictures. Experiment with different kinds of papers and colored inks.

Supplies

Water-based printing ink
Brayer (roller)
Foam
Cardboard for base

Scissors
Glue
Colored paper
Newspaper scrap paper

What do you see?—Ana, 9

Floating leaves.—Valin, 9

Try these, too!

Stencil It!

Like Matisse, paint colors through stenciled shapes. Cut your own stencils out of poster board. Hold your stencil in place on your picture. With a sponge, carefully apply thin paint in or around your stencil shape. You can also spray paint with a bottle. (Try not to let the paint go under the stencil.) Lift up your stencil! Repeat it to make fun patterns.

Make Your Own Book

Assemble your prints into a handmade book. Make different prints or drawings for the pages. Punch holes along the edges of the papers. Attach the pages by stringing them together with yarn or ribbon. Matisse wrote words in his book *Jazz*. You can, too. Tell a story or write a poem.

Visit the seashore!—Ciara, 9

Dancing shapes.—Brett, 11

Look for the creature!—Raquel, 11

AMAZING ABSTRACT SCULPTURE

ALEXANDER CALDER

The artist Alexander Calder invented an exciting new kind of abstract sculpture with movable parts, called the mobile. Calder's imagination was sparked when he visited his friend Piet Mondrian's art studio. Calder wondered what it would look like if the colorful rectangles in Mondrian's paintings could move. Later, Calder attached motors to his own artworks that set shapes in motion. Calder was not satisfied. He wanted the shapes to move freely on their own in surprising ways. So he hung wood pieces, metal shapes, glass, and other materials from wires. The playful shapes twirled round and round as air flowed past them.

Take a look at this standing mobile. Imagine the circles moving around. You might see a make-believe creature, or the planets, a moon, and the sun. Everywhere Calder went, he brought tools so he could make sculptures. Some of these artworks were so small they fit in the palm of his hand. Others were made of gigantic steel shapes that hung from the ceilings of huge buildings. Calder captured the movement of the universe in thousands of brilliant mobiles.

Look at this **standing mobile**. Imagine it in **motion**.

- What comes to mind when you **look** at this artwork? What makes you say that?
- What do all the **circles** remind you of? Find the large **red circle**. What does that look like to you?
- What could the **curved black shape** on the bottom be?
- Find shapes that look like a **face**, an **eye**, or a **body**. **Imagine**. What kind of **person** or **creature** might this be? What else do you see?

Myxomatose, 1953
Sheet metal and rod, 101 x 161 inches
Private collection

- Describe the **feeling** of this **sculpture**. Is it happy, sad, funny, or silly? What other words would you use?
- Picture this **mobile moving**. How do you think the parts would **move**? Which shapes might **spin** around? Which might **bounce**?
- How do you suppose the artist **created** this artwork? What **materials** do you think he used?
- Make up a **title** for this sculpture. Why would you call it that?

Compare this artwork to all the others in this book. What about this one is **different**? What **similarities** can you find?

Build it, bend it, twist it, shape it!
Construct all kinds of amazing abstract sculptures.

Marvelous Mobiles

Make a mobile using paper shapes, wire, and other decorative materials.

Like Calder, get ideas for your sculpture by thinking about things that are in motion all around you. Look up! Notice the moon and sun or the clouds as they move in the sky. Watch a kite or leaves blow in the wind. Spin yourself around! Then make a playful mobile. Hang it from the ceiling and watch it move!

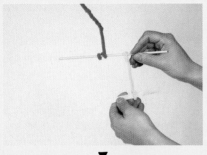

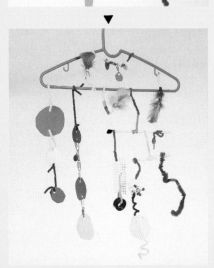

1. Start with a clothes hanger. Find a place where you can hang it up as you work. Or place it on a table.

2. Hang sticks from the hanger. Tie them on with pipe cleaners, wire, or string.

3. Cut shapes out of paper, cardboard, or foam sheets. Punch holes into the shapes.

4. Hang shapes from your mobile with wire, pipe cleaners, or string.

5. Add other materials such as beads, seashells, plastic flowers, or anything else you can think of. Calder attached glass pieces, wooden parts, and even broken pottery to his mobiles. Be creative. Think of different ways you can attach things.

6. Balance your mobile as you work. Move pieces around and watch what happens as you add and change things.

7. Watch your mobile in motion. Notice that its shadows move, too!

Supplies

Clothes hanger
Wooden dowels
Wire or pipe cleaners
String

Colored paper, cardboard, or colored foam
Decorative materials such as feathers, beads, seashells
Scissors

When everything goes right, a mobile is a piece of poetry that dances with the joy of life and surprises. —Alexander Calder

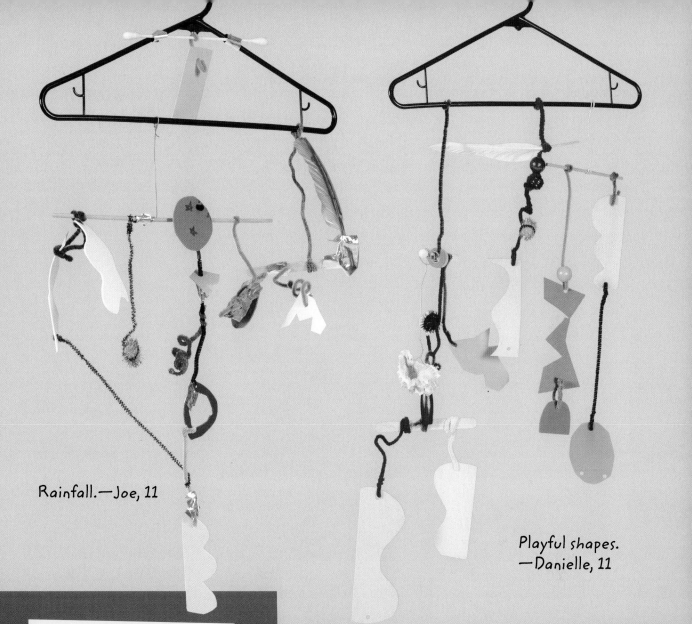

Rainfall.—Joe, 11

Playful shapes.
—Danielle, 11

Try this, too!

Wire Lines

Almost everywhere Calder went, he carried a spool of wire and pliers with him. He twisted wire to make whimsical animals, people, and designs. He called his creations "drawing in space." Try it yourself. Bend wire or pipe cleaners. Curl it around your finger to make a coil. Create loops or zigzags. Make a design with lines that wiggle, spiral, and stretch across space or form a person or animal. Staple your wire sculpture to a wooden stand.

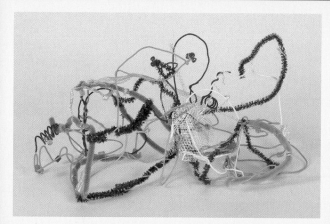

Lines of the ocean.—Ashley and Jasmine, 11

Build It!

More art inspired by Calder

Build a sculpture out of cardboard shapes and other materials without using glue! In addition to mobiles, Calder made gigantic standing sculptures called stabiles. Some look like huge insects or creatures. Others are completely abstract. Many of Calder's huge stabiles were built outdoors in cities, so that people can walk under and around them. Make your own construction. Pretend it is a model for a large outdoor sculpture.

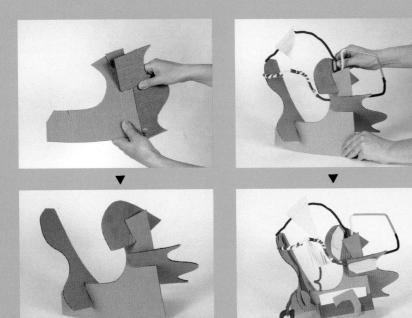

Supplies

Corrugated cardboard
Pipe cleaners or wire
Wooden dowels
Decorative materials
    such as string,
    feathers, beads,
    straws
Scissors
Decorative paper
Glue stick
Painting supplies (optional)

1. Cut shapes out of corrugated cardboard. Cut out geometric shapes such as triangles, rectangles, and circles. Or cut out curvy shapes. (You can ask an adult to help.)

2. Cut slits into the edges of each piece of cardboard. Make the slits about one inch long.

3. Build without glue! Attach cardboard pieces by sliding the slits together.

4. Add pipe cleaners or sticks. Poke them into the cardboard flutes. (These are the small holes along the edge of the cardboard.)

5. Tie it! Twist it! String it! Add other materials such as straws, string, ribbon, beads, feathers, or anything else. You can attach things by twisting them onto pipe cleaners. String beads onto wires or ribbon.

6. Color it! Paint the cardboard. Or glue colored paper or wrapping paper to it. Don't forget to look at all sides of the sculpture as you work.

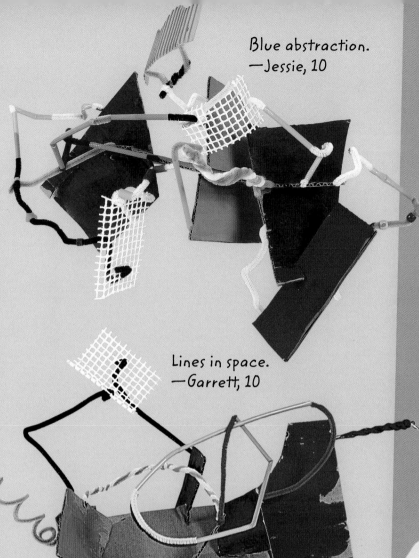

Blue abstraction.
—Jessie, 10

Lines in space.
—Garrett, 10

Abstract Animal Creations

Calder made thousands of playful animal sculptures. Once he made a circus filled with animals he built from fabric scraps, wood, and wire pieces. Construct your own animal. It does not have to look real. Build it with cardboard shapes for the body, head, and legs. Decorate it with feathers, pipe cleaners, or anything else you find. Add eyes, ears, and a tail. What will you call your creature?

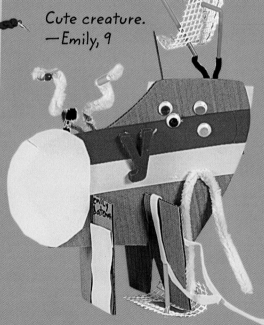

Cute creature.
—Emily, 9

Styrofoam Construction

You can also make a construction with Styrofoam pieces. Join Styrofoam shapes together by poking toothpicks or sticks into each piece. Add wire, straws, stickers, feathers, and other materials to your abstract creation. This kind of sculpture—when you add one material to another—is called a construction.

Girl fun.—Raquel and Erin, 11

NATURE UP CLOSE

GEORGIA O'KEEFFE

Take a close look at this painting by the artist Georgia O'Keeffe. You might see a wild explosion, a hot flame, or a beautiful design. Look again. When O'Keeffe made this picture, she painted a gorgeous gigantic flower! Instead of drawing a flower in an ordinary way, O'Keeffe looked at the flower and then let colors, shapes, and lines flow from her imagination onto her abstract painting.

In real life, flowers are small, but O'Keeffe painted them larger than life. The red-hot blossoms fill up her huge canvas. It is as if you are a bee or a butterfly sitting in its petals, seeing the flower way up close. Imagine. What would it feel like to sit in this flower? What would you see as you travel around all these shapes? O'Keeffe painted more than two hundred colorful abstract flower paintings—sunflowers, petunias, poppies, daffodils, orchids, calla lilies, and more. Many people loved O'Keeffe's stunning paintings, and she became famous for them.

What do you **see** in this picture?

- What does this picture **remind you** of? What makes you say that?
- **Look** at the picture in different ways. Turn it **upside down** or **sideways**. Now what do you **see**?
- Georgia O'Keeffe got the idea for this picture by looking at a **flower**. What type of flower might this be? How would you describe it?
- **Imagine.** If you were a **bee or butterfly** sitting in this flower, what would that be like? Travel all around the **blossoms**. What might you **feel**? How would it **smell**? What would it be like to be in this picture?

Red Canna, c. 1923
oil on canvas mounted on Masonite
36 x 29 7/8 inches
Collection of The University of Arizona
Museum of Art, Tucson

- How is this flower **different** from the way most flowers look in real life? What parts of the flower are not shown in this painting?
- What words would you use to describe the **feeling** of this picture? Is it calm or explosive? Joyful, sad, angry, or some other word?
- Let your eyes wander in and around the painting. What kinds of **lines** and **shapes** do you see? Can you find any **patterns**?
- How would you describe the **colors**? Are they **hot** or **cool**? Which colors are **light** or **dark**?
- Make up a **title** for this picture. Why would you choose this name?

What is your **favorite flower?**

Flowers, seashells, mountains, oceans, and more. Capture the beauty of nature in abstract paintings.

Gorgeous Gigantic Flowers

Make art inspired by O'Keeffe

Paint an abstract picture of a giant flower. Sunflowers, roses, poppies, daffodils, orchids, calla lilies! O'Keeffe was fascinated with the beauty of flowers. She looked closely into the flower's petals. Then she let the colors and shapes that she saw flow freely from her mind onto her paintings. What is your favorite flower? Paint it into a fun-filled abstract design.

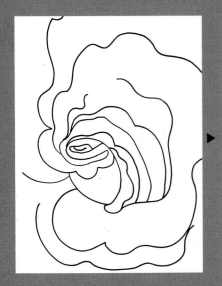 ▶ 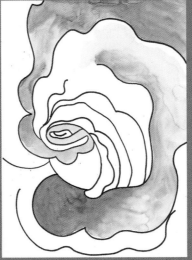 ▶

1. Find a flower for your artwork. Get a real one or use an artificial plastic flower. You can also find pictures on the Internet or in magazines. I love roses!

2. Look into the flower. Draw what you see with a pencil. Do not make it look exactly real. Instead, turn your flower into a design. Let your eyes wander around the shapes of the petals as you draw.

3. Draw it really large. Fill up the entire paper. Let the petals and shapes go right off the edges.

4. Make designs. I filled my picture with curves that swirl around.

5. Add detcils. Look into the center of your flower. You can draw the stamen or the pistil. Add lines and shapes you see on the petals or leaves.

6. Go over your pencil lines with non-water-soluble marker.

7. Color it in with watercolor or tempera paint. Change the colors. I made a blue and orange-red rose. Blend one color into another. Go from light to dark by varying the amount of water you mix in with your paint. (Tip: Add water to keep the paint thin so you do not cover up your lines.)

8. After the paint dries, go back over the lines with marker again if needed.

Supplies

Paper
Painting supplies
Non-water-soluble markers
Pencil

Flower swirl.—Nicole, 10

Up-close designs.—Daniel, 11

Rainbow petals.—Brittanie, 10

Lots of colors.—Roberta, 11

Try this, too!

Spectacular Leaves

O'Keeffe loved nature. She saw beauty in the patterns of leaves and painted those, too. Find a leaf. Take a close look at it. Draw the shape of the leaf really big. Let it go right off the edge of your paper. Then add lines and patterns that you see on the leaf. Isn't it pretty? Instead of painting it green, you can paint it rainbow colors or any way you want. Turn your leaf into an abstract work of art.

Fiery leaf-flower.—Raquel, 11, Erin, 13, and Timmy, 13

Abstract Nature

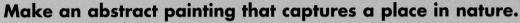

See beauty like O'Keeffe

Make an abstract painting that captures a place in nature.
Wherever O'Keeffe lived, she painted the beauty around her in her abstract pictures. Living in New Mexico, she painted the open land of the desert. In New York City, she captured the bright lights of city skyscrapers. Look around where you live. Spectacular trees, sky, land, or water! Capture the nature around you in an abstract painting.

▼

▼

1. Choose a place for your artwork. Here are some ideas: the seaside, a river, a lake, mountains, a winding road, a forest, trees, the sky.

2. Look around. Notice the shapes and patterns in nature. I live near the ocean. At the beach, I see curving waves and patterns of lines in sand. In the mountains, you might see rolling hills. Look up into trees. Do you see a web of lines?

3. Using crayon, draw an abstract picture of a place. Do not make everything look real. Draw simple flowing shapes and lines. I drew swirling lines for my ocean. I filled my sky with wobbly clouds that make a pretty pattern.

4. Color it in. Do not paint real colors. Instead, fill your picture with any kinds of colors you imagine. I painted pink clouds and an orange sky.

5. Blend it. Make colors go from light to dark by mixing in more white. Make colors warmer by adding red or yellow. Make cool colors by adding blue.

6. Add pastel or crayons. After your painting dries, it is fun to blend pastels over your colors. You can also go back over your crayon lines.

Supplies

Paper
Crayons
Painting supplies
Pastels (optional)

I found I could say things with colors and shapes that I couldn't say any other way—things I had no words for.—Georgia O'Keeffe

Island waters.—Erica, 12

From up above.—Roy, 12

Flowing river.—Rafael, 12

Try this, too!

Collect It!

O'Keeffe took nature walks and picked up interesting things she found along the way, such as rocks, wood, flowers, shells, and more. What will you collect? With an adult, stroll along the seashore, hike in the woods, or go for a walk on your street. Collect a seashell, a twig, or anything else. Look at it closely. Make an abstract drawing of your object. Draw the patterns and shapes you see. For example, draw the swirls of a seashell. Then paint it fun colors.

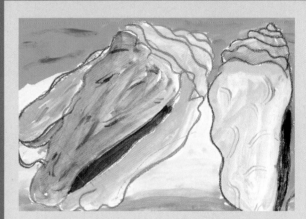

Hear the ocean?—Natasha, 12

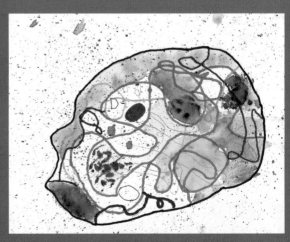

I found coral!—Chris, 10

PAINT IT OUT!

ARSHILE GORKY

An energetic swoosh of paint! Bold colors! Wild lines that swirl across the painting! The artist Arshile Gorky let all kinds of lines, shapes, and colors flow freely from his mind onto this exciting painting. Let your eyes travel around the picture. You might see funny faces, creatures, plants, or a wild river. Gorky got the idea for this painting by studying nature when he stayed in the Connecticut countryside. He also remembered the beautiful gardens from his homeland, Armenia, where he grew up. As you can see, Gorky did not copy nature. Instead he painted from his imagination to create an abstract landscape filled with designs.

You do not have to color inside the lines to be a great artist. Gorky let the watery paint drip all over and colors blend together. It seems like Gorky painted quickly, but he actually painted carefully and often made sketches to plan his pictures. His style of art, when the artist releases feelings with energetic brushstrokes and vibrant colors, is called abstract expressionism.

Imagine. If you could be in this **abstract painting,** what would it be like?

- Travel through the painting. Look around. What do you **see**?
- Look closely. Can you find something that looks like a **face**, a **creature**, a **bird**? What else do you notice?
- Play a **looking game** with friends. **Describe in detail** something that you spot in the painting. Without pointing, see if they can **find it**. Give **visual clues**. For example, I see a funny face with a red eye and a brown one. Can you find it?
- What words would you use to **describe this picture**? Is it wild or calm, confused or joyful? Messy or neat? What other words might you use?

Water of the Flowery Mill, 1944
oil on canvas, height 42¼ inches,
width 48¾ inches (107.3 x 123.8 cm)
The Metropolitan Museum of Art,
New York City

- Notice all the **lines, shapes, and colors**. What words would you use to describe them? For example, are they curved or straight? Round or sharp? Bright or dull?
- Now look at the **entire picture**. What **title** would you give it? Explain your choice.
- Picture the **artist at work** making this picture. What do you notice about the way it is painted? Can you find any places where he let the paint **drip**? Can you find any areas where he **blended colors**?

Compare this painting to Matisse's picture on page 21. How are these artworks **different**? What about them is **similar**?

Paint it! Press it! Drip it! Surprise yourself!
Release your imagination and emotions through abstract expressionist painting.

Wild Lines

Make art inspired by Gorky

Draw a continuous line with oil pastels. Then paint in and around your drawing with watercolor. Like Gorky, travel into your mind. See what comes out as your hand moves around the paper. Let all kinds of lines and colors flow onto your picture. There is no such thing as a mistake! Let your imagination be free. This kind of art—when you draw continuously without thinking—is called automatic drawing.

▼

▼

1. Draw a line with crayons or oil pastels. Don't lift your crayon as you draw. Don't stop to think about what you are drawing. Draw slowly. Watch the lines that come out as you draw them.

2. Create different kinds of lines. You can make zig-zags and curls, wiggly lines and straight ones. (Tip: Press hard with your crayon so the lines will show up clearly.)

3. What do you see? Look into your lines. Turn your paper upside down or sideways. Look at it in different ways. You might see faces, animals, a roller coaster, or fun-filled designs.

4. Lightly paint with watercolors over and around the lines when your drawing is completed. Notice how the oil pastel lines show through. (Tip: Add lots of water so you do not cover up your drawing. Use contrasting colors. For example, yellow paint next to red lines shows up well.)

5. Title your picture. I call mine *Wild Garden of Color*.

Supplies

Crayons or oil pastels
Paper
Watercolor painting
   supplies

In my art I often draw our garden and re-create its precious greenery and life.—Arshile Gorky

Loops and zigzags.—Alex, 9

Flowing lines.—Dana, 9

Out of my imagination!—Mallorie, 9

Lines Have Feelings, Too

Energetic, wild, joyful, or free! Instead of drawing a person or a face, Gorky showed his emotions by painting lines and colors. Try it yourself! Make an abstract painting to show a feeling. You might draw jagged lines for anger or swirling ones for happy. Write the feeling on the back. See if people can guess the emotion you painted.

Crazy confusion.—Sean, 9

What's in a Name?

Some abstract artists got ideas by painting the lines of the letters in their name. Fold a sheet of paper in half. On one side of the paper, along the edge of the fold, neatly paint your name. While the paint is wet, carefully fold the paper together and press against your wet painting. Open it up. Paint back into your picture to create an abstract design.

Can you find my name?—Santiago, 9

Feel the Paint

Make an abstract painting without using a paintbrush.

Swoosh it, spatter it, smear it all over! Gorky freely let wet paint blend and drip in an energetic explosion of color. Express yourself with paint! To free yourself, instead of using a paintbrush, apply paint with sticks, cotton balls, and other fun stuff. Release your energy as you smear, stamp, scrape, spill, and spray paint.

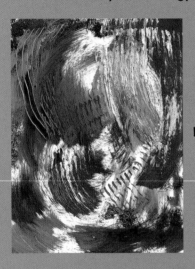 ▶ 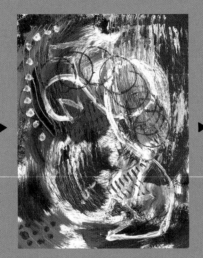 ▶

1. Find things you can use to apply paint. Collect sponges, cotton balls, sticks, cotton swabs, plastic forks, combs, spray bottles, cardboard paper rolls, or anything else. Ask an adult to help.

2. Set up your paints. It can be helpful to limit your painting to one of these combinations so the colors don't get muddy: red, purple, and blue; or yellow, orange, and red; or blue, green, and purple. Pour your colors on separate spots on a plastic plate. Also use white.

3. Cover your paper with paint. What tool can you use to cover large areas on your paper? I smeared on paint with sponges. Messy fun!

4. Make your mark! Apply paint with the tools you have chosen. Experiment! Here are some ideas: Scrape into paint with combs, plastic forks, and sticks to make lines. Stamp out circles with cardboard rolls or print rectangles with sponges.

Drip paint from a stick. Sprinkle paint from a toothbrush. Squirt from a turkey baster or spray bottle. Roll paint on with a golf ball or marble dipped in paint.

5. Title your abstract painting. I call mine *Night Storm*.

Supplies

Objects to paint with (such as sponges, sticks, toothbrush, cotton swabs, paper roller, plastic fork, comb, cardboard paper towel rolls, turkey baster)
Paint
Paper
Paper plate for palette

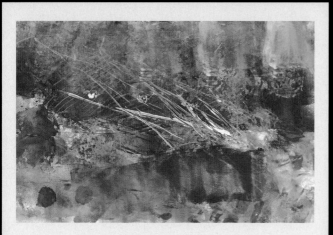

The way I feel.—Peter, 9

Starry night.—David, 14

Heart hopes.—Jasmine, 14

Try these, too!

Blow It!

Abstract expressionist painters invented fun ways to make paint move. Gorky let paint drip. Others picked up their paintings and swooshed wet paint around. I paint by blowing it with a straw. Brush watery paint onto paper. Blow through a straw, and watch the paint move.

Fireworks!—Freddy, 7

Drip It! Rip It!

Be an action painter! The abstract artist Jackson Pollock became famous for his drip paintings. His wife, Lee Krasner, made artworks by ripping up her old paintings. Make a painting filled with designs. Drip paint onto it from a stick. Now rip your painting into pieces! Glue the pieces to another paper to make a new picture, and add more paint if you like.

I love abstract art!—Mia, 8

Print It! Press It!

Make It Abstract

Create an abstract picture by making a monoprint. Art is an adventure. Surprise yourself! Make unusual abstract expressionist pictures with printmaking. Apply ink or paint to a plastic sheet, then press a paper on it. This kind of printmaking—when you make just *one* copy—is called a monoprint. Your print can be completely abstract, or it might remind you of a feeling, a season, or something else.

1. Get a clean sheet of heavy plastic. This will be your printing plate. You can also cut a rectangle out of a large disposable plastic plate. (For safety, ask an adult to put tape along the edges so they are not sharp.)

2. Set up your colors. Squeeze several colors of ink or paint on a separate plate so you will have colors to choose from.

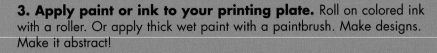
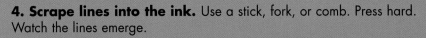

3. Apply paint or ink to your printing plate. Roll on colored ink with a roller. Or apply thick wet paint with a paintbrush. Make designs. Make it abstract!

4. Scrape lines into the ink. Use a stick, fork, or comb. Press hard. Watch the lines emerge.

5. Cut out shapes from scrap paper. Roll ink onto them or leave them plain. Then carefully place them on your wet printing plate face up. (They will block the ink.)

6. Place a sheet of paper over your inked-up printing plate. Gently press with your hand or a brayer. Lift up the paper to see your print. Surprise! (Tip: As you work, do not let the paint or ink dry before you print it.)

7. Draw back into your picture when it is dry if you want.

Supplies

Plastic sheet
Water-based printing ink
    or tempera paint
Brayer (roller)
Brushes
Paper
Stick, fork, or comb

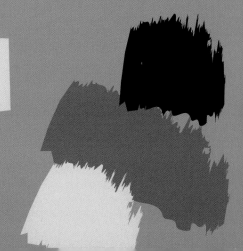

Deep in the ocean.—Khavir, 12

Red creatures.—Brianna, 12

What do you see?—Courtney, 12

Fold It!

Some modern artists liked to make art that would surprise them. It is fun to make a picture without knowing how it will turn out or controlling what it will be. See for yourself! Make a wet gooey painting. You can drip paint onto it. While it is still wet, fold it in half. Press your wet painting together. Unfold it. What do you see? Is it a butterfly, a face, or something else?

I love paint!—Edgar, 9

So I made two pictures!—Edgar, 9

Pablo Picasso
Spanish, 1881–1973

Pablo Picasso was born in Malaga, Spain. His father was a painter and teacher who encouraged Picasso to be an artist. As a teenager, Picasso went to art school and painted all day. He showed amazing talent.

In 1904, Picasso moved to Paris, where he met other artists. He worked with his close friend Georges Braque who was also a painter. They created a new kind of art called Cubism. In their abstract paintings, people and places seem to be broken apart and things seem to move and shift. Instead of painting people the way they really look, Picasso painted imaginative people to show strong emotions. For example, a sad person was painted entirely blue! A calm girl might be painted pink and yellow. During the 1930s and 1940s, Picasso expressed his feelings about World War II and the Spanish civil war. His great masterpiece *Guernica* shows crying women and animals suffering during wartime.

After World War II, Picasso moved to the south of France. He continued to invent unusual ways of making art. He collected scrap materials, newspapers, toys, and junk and used them to make playful collages and sculptures. He also created ceramics, prints, book illustrations, and set designs. A creative genius, Picasso is considered one of the greatest modern artists worldwide.

Fernand Léger
French, 1881–1955

Fernand Léger was born in Normandy, France, the son of a cattle breeder. As a teenager, he showed creative talent, so his family sent him to study and work with an architect. A few years later, he moved to Paris and earned a living as an architectural draftsman. He decided to attend art school there.

Inspired by Pablo Picasso, Léger painted abstract pictures in a Cubist style. In Léger's paintings, everything was broken up into lines and shapes that seem to move. Later, Léger began painting abstract pictures that captured the bright colors, lively shapes, and patterns he saw on city streets.

During World War I, Léger served in the army. When he returned to Paris, he showed the excitement of modern life in his art. In his pictures, you can see imaginary machines and people who look like robots! He also painted objects such as cups and bottles in his own unique style.

During World War II, Léger was forced to leave his country. He settled in New York City. Life in America inspired abstract paintings filled with color and energy. After the war, he returned home. He painted lively pictures of people at work and at play. He also made set designs, stained glass windows, and murals. He died on his farm in France in 1955. Today, Léger is remembered as one of the most important modern painters.

Henri Matisse
French, 1869–1954

Henri Matisse grew up in a village in France. Matisse did not realize he had a talent for art until he was a young man. He studied law and worked in an office. Bored with his job, he attended drawing classes. When he was twenty, he was recovering from an illness and he began to paint. About a year later, he went to Paris to study painting.

Soon, Matisse began experimenting with new ways of painting. He led a group of artists who painted with bright, bold colors. In Matisse's paintings, you'll see blue dancers, pink landscapes, and a woman with a green face! Some people were shocked by his unusual art. Matisse and his group were called *les fauves*, French for "the wild beasts."

Matisse believed art should be happy. He painted beautiful women, colorful flowers, dancers, and nature. Everywhere he went he painted the beauty around him. He traveled to Spain, Algeria, Morocco, Germany, and the south of France. His pictures are filled with bright colors, patterns, and lively decorations.

In 1909, Matisse bought a house in Nice, France. There he made prints, sculptures, and books, and designed a chapel. In his old age, Matisse became bedridden. Unable to paint, he made colorful cutouts. Today Matisse is one of the most popular artists in the world.

Alexander Calder
American, 1898–1976

Alexander Calder was born in Lawton, Pennsylvania. His father and grandfather were famous sculptors, and his mother was a painter. As a child, he collected scrap materials and made toys and dolls out of them. When Calder grew up, he worked as an engineer. Later he decided to study art at the Art Students League in New York. He earned money as an illustrator drawing animals and circus performers. In 1926, Calder moved to Paris. There he created one of his most famous projects, the Calder *Circus*. He sculpted circus performers, animals, and clowns out of fabric, wood, and wire. Then he acted out a circus performance with the movable pieces, and many people came to see it.

Calder moved back to the United States in 1934. He got a job in Wisconsin designing toys that moved. Calder made art wherever he went. He carried a spool of wire and twisted wire lines to make hundreds of playful animals and people. He invented the mobile—exciting sculptures with movable parts. Later, Calder created gigantic steel sculptures called stabiles. Made of abstract shapes, some look like insects or animals. Beginning in 1954, Calder began splitting his time between France and the United States. Calder lived a happy life and made more than 16,000 artworks. He made sculptures, rugs, stage sets, paintings, prints, jewelry, and utensils, and painted an airplane and a race car! He is one of America's most popular artists.

Georgia O'Keeffe
American, 1887–1986

Georgia O'Keeffe grew up on a farm in Wisconsin. As a child she took art lessons. By age twelve, she decided she wanted to be an artist. When she was seventeen, she studied art in Chicago. Later, she went to school in New York City and taught art in Virginia and South Carolina.

In 1918, O'Keeffe moved to New York City. She exhibited her work at an art gallery called 291. The famous photographer Alfred Stieglitz ran it. The two married in 1924. O'Keeffe captured the beauty around her in each place she lived. Instead of painting realistically, O'Keeffe filled her pictures with abstract shapes, colors, and patterns. In the city, she painted skyscrapers and bright lights with geometric shapes. During the summers, when O'Keeffe lived in the mountains, she painted colorful lakes, skies, mountains, and barns. She became most famous for her close-ups of flowers filled with flowing designs.

In 1929, O'Keeffe visited New Mexico, and from then on she spent part of every year there. She painted the deserts and canyons. A few years later, she moved to New Mexico permanently. At age seventy-one, she traveled the world. When she grew older, she began to lose her eyesight, so she worked in clay. O'Keeffe died at age ninety-eight. A popular American artist, her home in New Mexico is now a museum.

Arshile Gorky
American, born in Armenia, 1904–1948

Arshile Gorky was born in Turkish Armenia. His name was Vosdanig Manoog Adoian. As an adult, he changed it to Arshile Gorky. During his childhood, his father left for America to flee from war, and his mother died. At age fifteen, with little money, Gorky moved to America and joined his family in Rhode Island. To earn a living, Gorky did odd jobs and later taught art. Gorky sometimes barely had enough money for food or paint supplies. But no matter what, Gorky made art. When he couldn't buy paints, he used a pencil and paper to draw.

In 1925, Gorky moved to New York City. There he taught himself to paint. He studied the paintings of famous artists such as Picasso and Léger and copied their styles. Gorky made murals for the WPA, a program that hired artists to make public artworks.

Eventually, Gorky discovered his own unique way of painting. In his abstract pictures, he expressed his feelings and imagination. Gorky painted flowing lines and splashes of bold color. He let the paint drip and colors blend. He spent summers in Connecticut, where he enjoyed the outdoors. The animals and plants he saw there appear in his abstract paintings. Gorky became well known and occasionally sold paintings. During the 1940s, Gorky became ill, and he died young. Even though he had a difficult life, Gorky was a great painter, and he inspired many artists.

About the Author

Joyce Raimondo, creator of the Art Explorer series, is director of Imagine That! Art Education, specializing in helping children access the arts. As a visiting author to schools and a consultant, she teaches children how to look at famous artworks and use art history as a springboard for their own creativity. Her clients include the Pollock-Krasner House and Study Center in East Hampton, Children's Television Workshop, and numerous museums.

Joyce is the author of The Museum of Modern Art's acclaimed Art Safari series of children's books, kits, and online program. From 1992–2000, she served as Family Programs Coordinator at MoMA in New York, where she created programs that teach children and adults how to enjoy art.

A painter and sculptor, Joyce Raimondo has had her illustrations featured in such publications as the *New York Times* and the *Boston Globe*. Her television appearances include *Blues' Clues, Fox Breakfast Time,* and *NBC News*, among others. She lives in East Hampton, New York. Visit her on the web at www.joyceraimondo.com.

Joyce and Buddy

Acknowledgments

As director of Imagine That! Art Education, I implement workshops designed to teach children how to enjoy art history. I ask students to describe what they see in famous artworks and follow up with their own creations. Much of the children's art featured in this book was made during these workshops.

A special thanks to the children who contributed artworks to this book. Gratitude is given to my editors, Julie Mazur and Laaren Brown, for bringing clarity to the fifth volume in the Art Explorer series. I am also thankful to Ed Miller, the designer, who created the book's lively graphics, and to Frank Roccanova and Kathleen Bifulco for their photographic contributions.

Grateful acknowledgment is due to the schools who participated in this project: Amagansett, Covert, John F. Kennedy Middle School, Montauk, Phillips Avenue, Project Most, Quogue, Roslyn Middle School, Southampton, Springs, and Syosset. Special thanks is given to those who arranged the programs: Mary Jane Aceri, Tim Bryden, Diane Fierro, Rebecca Morgan, Cathleen Musick, Liz Paris, and Anne Sueiro; and to the art teachers whose students produced works for this book: Ginger Anderson, Debbie Cantalupo, Kristen Daly, Laurie Learner, Cindy Miller, Lois Reboli, and Paul Saltzman. Appreciation is given to the Nassau and Suffolk Boards of Cooperative Education, which funded many of these workshops.

Together, let's keep art in the schools!

by Kevin, 7

by Rachel, 10

48